YOUR KNOWLEDGE HAS VALUE

- We will publish your bachelor's and
  master's thesis, essays and papers

- Your own eBook and book -
  sold worldwide in all relevant shops

- Earn money with each sale

Upload your text at www.GRIN.com
and publish for free

Therese .

The Many Names of Leni Riefenstahl

GRIN Verlag

Bibliografische Information der Deutschen Nationalbibliothek:

Die Deutsche Bibliothek verzeichnet diese Publikation in der Deutschen National-
bibliografie; detaillierte bibliografische Daten sind im Internet über http://dnb.d-
nb.de/ abrufbar.

Imprint:

Copyright © 2012 GRIN Verlag GmbH
Druck und Bindung: Books on Demand GmbH, Norderstedt Germany
ISBN: 978-3-656-27248-9

This book at GRIN:

http://www.grin.com/en/e-book/201085/the-many-names-of-leni-riefenstahl

The many Names of Leni Riefenstahl

An Essay on filmmaker and photographer Leni Riefenstahl

Inhaltsverzeichnis

Introduction

'I want to become something quite great'- Leni Riefenstahl (Bach 2007, p. 9).

Leni Riefenstahl has been, and still is, a much-discussed person. She has been called many things, and given many labels.
She has been called a liar, a man-eater, a Nazi, an extraordinary talent and a genius.

She was an actress, director, dancer, filmmaker and photographer.
In her career, she has done everything between making Nazi propaganda films, to taking photos of Mick Jagger, to photograph unknown tribes in Africa.

Leni had many talents, but her great passion, and what she is best known for is her great filmmaking.
She was the brain behind the masterpiece of propaganda films *Triumph of the Will* [1935], which she made for Hitler and the Nazi Party before World War 2.
She was a close friend to Hitler before and during the war, and as described in Bach (2007 p.388) she is probably best known as "Hitler's Filmmaker".

She continued her friendship and collaboration with Hitler long after it was a well-known fact that Hitler was responsible for an unimaginable Genocide.
There have been many speculations on why she stayed close with Hitler, which raises the questions; was Leni supportive or neutral to the regime? Was she forced in any way? Or was she simply loyal to her country, and to her friend Der Führer himself?

To even begin to understand her complex character and her work, one must know her full story. The way from her adolescence in Berlin, until she turned in to be one of the world's most famous filmmakers and photographers, with the help from her great talent, and of Adolf Hitler.

Background

Leni's birth name was Hélène Amalie Bertha Riefenstahl. She was born on August
the 22,1902, in a district called Wedding in Berlin.
Her father, Alfred Theodor Paul Riefenstahl, was a plumber by profession. Later in
life he became a successful businessman (Taschen 2001, p.296).
Her mothers name was Bertha Ida Riefenstahl, and Leni had one younger brother,
Heinz (Bach, 2007).

Leni seemed to have a good relationship with her mother, and the two Riefenstahl
women often went behind Alfred's back together. As described in Taschen (2001, p.
296) Bertha and Leni used to secretly go to the cinema together when Alfred was
away on hunting trips.
Bach (2007, p.12) shows that there has appeared strong evidence that her mother's
father was Jewish, meaning that Leni herself was part Jewish. Later, Hitler would put
a stop to any speculations and rumours about Leni's family background.

Wedding in Berlin was a hard place to grow up. It was a district in the industrial
edges of Berlin, a labour district. Families lived in cramped one-room flats. Death by
Tuberculosis and suicide was daily happenings in Wedding (Bach, 2007 p.11).

Leni's adolescence seems to be very much marked by her father. Alfred was an
authority figure who ruled his family with an iron hand and strict discipline.
He never had much fate in his daughter's skills. As quoted in Bach (2007,p.21) he
once told his daughter: 'Personally I am convinced that you have little talent, and will
never be more than mediocre'.

At the age of 16 Leni attended dancing lessons, paid for by her mother, kept a secret
from her father. She was very confidant, and determined to do something great with
her life. After a while she was dancing in venues all over Germany, and she also got
bookings in Prague and Zurich (Taschen, 2001).

She was a beauty at this stage; attending beauty contests, and making men fall in love with her. She had many boyfriends, and left behind many broken hearts (Bach 2007, p.22).

According to Bach (2007, p.22) especially one of her admirers suffered a hard fate. Walter Lubovski was a young Jewish boy who was madly in love with her, and Leni turned him into some sort of a love slave. Leni and her girlfriends made him cross-dress and other humiliating things, until he slashed his wrists at Leni's family's country house. Leni shoved him, still bleeding, under a sofa to prevent discovery by Alfred.
Walter ended up in a mental institution and Leni reacted to his fate by saying, 'He never forgot me as long as he lived' (Bach 2007, p. 22).

Later, Leni started a secret love affair with the tennis player Otto Froizheim. As described in Bach (2007, p.23) the relationship was unhealthy from the start. After loosing her virginity to Otto, he tossed her a 20-dollar bill and said;' If you get pregnant, you can use this to get rid of it' (Bach, 2007 p.23).
The affair lasted for two years, and next on the list was a young Jewish bank director named Harry Sokal.

After the affair with Sokal, Leni had affairs to many different athletes, cameramen, crewmembers, directors and actors.
The affairs were often beneficial for her career, but in 1944 she married Lieutenant Peter Jacob, out of love (Bach, 2007).
They got divorced two years later, and Leni didn't remarry until the day of her 101th birthday. Then she married her 40 years younger assistant, Horst Kettner. Leni and Kettner stayed married until she died in her sleep a few months later (Bach, 2007).

Films

The first film she starred in was the documentary *Ways to strength and beauty* [1925]. Leni has later denied ever being in the film. Bach (2007, p.4) suggests that this was because the film didn't give her enough credit.

After that she starred in a series of mountain films for Arnold Frank, and the film *The White Hell of Pitz Palu* [1929], gave her international success (Bach, 2007).

The film *The Blue Light* from 1932, which she co-directed and starred in, became her big breakthrough.
This was the film that got Hitler interested in Leni and her work (Bach, 2007, p.91). The film got re-released in 1938, this time with no Jewish names in it. It has been said that this was to Leni's recognition (Bach, 2007, p.240).

Triumph of the Will and filmmaking for Der Führer

To Hitler, Leni was the perfection of a German woman. She was multi- talented, healthy and athletic. She had the talent of a man, and the shapes of a pin-up model.

Bach (2007, p.91), describes that, according to Hitler's adjutant Wilhelm Brückner, Hitler once said; ' The most beautiful thing I have ever seen was Leni Riefenstahl's dance on the sea in the *Holy Mountain*' [1926].
Bach (2007, p.93) shows that there have many been speculations on whether she had an intimate relationship with Hitler. According to people in Hitler's inner circle Leni tried to start an affair with him, but Hitler refused. According to Bach (2007, p. 93) she later in life told a friend; 'I would have become his mistress; had he asked, it would have been inevitable. I'm so glad he didn't'.

Hitler asked Leni to make the propaganda film *Triumph of the Will* [1935], and a star was born.
The film chronicles the Nazi Party Congress in Nuremberg, which took place in 1934 (Rother, 2003).
Taylor (1998, 162) describes the film as 'a superb example of documentary cinema art, and a masterpiece of film propaganda'.

The film starts with Hitler's airplane flying above the clouds, heading for Nuremberg. Hitler then appears as a saviour and a hero, to cheering crowds, giving the "Sieg Heil"

sign, and looking at him with stars in their eyes. It shows young boys playing and having fun, and a woman with her little daughter shaking Hitler's hand.
Later it shows marching troops, and the Swastika is an important image throughout the film. It's glorifying of a person on it's best.

After the success with *Triumph of the Will* [1935] she followed up by making yet another Nazi propaganda film called *A day of Freedom* [1935].
Hitler then asked her if she wanted to film the Olympic Games in Berlin, which resulted in her world famous film *Olympia* [1938] (Bach, 2007).

In 1940 Leni started the work on the film *Thiefland* [1954], which she both starred in and directed. She played the beautiful Gypsy dancer, Martha (Bach, 2007 p. 198).
Bach (2007, p. 201) shows that Leni needed Spanish looking extras for the film, and she found them in a "collection camp" called Maxglan for German Gypsies. The Gypsies were soon to be deported to Auschwitz.
Leni came to the camp together with a SS officer to choose the extras that she wanted for the film.
Bach (2007, p. 202) describes that Leni used her thumbs and forefingers to "frame" their faces as if looking through a viewfinder.

The Gypsies lived under very bad conditions on the set. They were under strict control by SS officers, and they were housed in stables during the filming. They were not paid directly, and after the filming they were sent to Auschwitz where most of them died. Bach (2007, p. 204) states that Leni called Maxglan a 'welfare- and care-camp',
Leni chose twenty-three Gypsies for the film, and the youngest was three months old (Bach, 2007).

Post -War

After the war Leni was in and out of courthouses for years. As Rother (2003) puts it;
'She can claim never to have been a member of the NSDAP (National Socialist

German Workers-or Nazi-Party), never to have committed a crime, and not to have vilified minorities in her films'.

She never got convicted for using slave labour in her film, even though the surviving Gypsies testified against her in court.

Bach (2007, p.202) points out that Leni denied ever to personally visit the camp Maxglan. After the war the surviving Gypsies from Maxglan testified that she was there, picking out the extras that she wanted for her film. As described in Bach (2007, p. 202) a then seventeen- year- old Gypsy girl named Rosa Winter recalled; 'We were all there in the camp. And then she came with the police and chose people'.

Another surviving Gypsy, Josef Reinhardt, then thirteen, recalled her tell an official; 'I can't take these people like this; they need to be re-clothed' (Bach, 2007 p. 203.).

Neither did Leni get convicted for being a Nazi propagandist.

Taylor, (1998 p.148) describes how 'The Führer preferred a complete separation of propaganda from art (this separation was to serve Leni Riefenstahl well in the early post-war years, because she felt able to claim that Triumph of the Will [1935] was "art" rather than "propaganda".'

In the end she was named "a fellow traveller" by the courts (Bach, 2007 p. 237).

After the war, many blacklisted her as a filmmaker and she started a new career as a photographer.

In 1974 she photographed Mick Jagger and his wife at the time, Bianca, for the Sunday Times (Bach, 2007).

Her most famous photography work is the photo books *The Last of the Nuba* [1973] and *The People of Kau* [1976], She lived with the Nuba tribe in Sudan when she was working, and the result was powerful images of the tribe people. The books were both international bestsellers.

Leni also had an interest for underwater photography and filming. In 1978 she made the book *Coral Gardens,* followed by *Wonder under Water* [1990].

On her 100th birthday she realised a short film called *Underwater Impressions* [2002] (Bach, 2007).

Conclusion

I didn't particularly enjoy watching *The Triumph of the Will* [1935], but I certainly understand how much talent that is behind it, and how powerful it was. Leni managed to create a great feeling of solidarity, respect and hope in the film. Hitler is glorified as a leader and saviour, which were much needed in Germany at the time. I think the film also shows Hitler as a "peoples man".
This film played such a big part in the war, and therefore it gives Leni a big role in the Holocaust.

In my opinion this is not something that Leni can possibly be held responsible for. She was blinded by the light of Der Führer, like the rest of Germany, and saw him as the way out of the economic despair that Germany was in.

It's the choices that she made later in her career, that brings up the questions of this woman's values and ideology.
Leni seemed to be a liar by nature. She lied about her own knowledge, lied about visiting places and lied about starring in films. She started lying to her father at a young age, something that could have followed her through life.

It seems like Leni had no feelings or sympathy for the Maxglan Gypsies.
She denied the visit of the camp, and stated that she had seen all the Gypsies after the war, which proves that she was a notorious liar. It's confusing that a woman this talented and famous would not make a wiser decision.
She was clearly there, and she saw the conditions the camp was in. I think the fact that she called Maxglan a 'welfare- and care- camp' shows either great stupidity or great selfishness and lack of sympathy. Considering her behaviour and comments when she visited the camp it's probably the last.
For a woman who was clearly loved and supported by her mother, her behaviour is very confusing.

Something to consider is that in the early 1900's the value of a human life was looked upon differently than it is today. Leni's childhood in Wedding, with sickness and death as a common thing, could have marked her.

Already as a young woman she showed lack of sympathy for others, when she clearly didn't care about the boy who tried to commit suicide because of her, in her living room.

Leni was always seeking for her father's acceptance and love, and she wanted him to be proud of what she had achieved. This may be some of the reason for her fascination for Hitler. Hitler gave Leni the amazing opportunity that became the breakthrough in her career. He was the biggest authority of all, and he admired her and believed in her, in a way her father never did.

Although the speculations have been many, nobody can know if she was a Nazi, maybe she didn't even know it herself. I think Leni certainly lived in strong denial; it's absolutely impossible that she didn't know what was going on during the war. She continued the denial and her lies for the rest of her life.

After studying Leni's character and her work, she comes across as a narcissistic and lying woman. She seemed to lack the ability to put herself in someone else's situation, and had a low respect for human life.
She was also an exceptionally talented, gifted and ambitious woman who could do anything she put her mind to.
The on-going discussion of whether she was a Nazi or not, can often overlook Leni's great work.

I think Leni's last film, *Underwater Impressions* [2002], is an absolutely beautiful film.
It's very peaceful and full of life at the same time. It has strong, positive and clear colours and relaxing music. I could have kept on watching it for way longer than it lasted. It couldn't get further away from her propaganda films. Maybe Leni found peace at last.

Bibliography:

Books:

Bach, S. (2007). *The Life and Work of Leni Riefenstahl,* London: Little Brown Book Group

Rother, R. (2003). *Leni Riefenstahl: The Seduction of Genius,* London: MPG Books Ltd

Tashen, A (2001) *Leni Riefenstahl, Five Lives,* New York: America LLC

Taylor, R (1998) *Film Propaganda, Soviet Russia and Nazi Germany,* London: I.B Tauris & Co Ltd

Documentaries:

Muller, R (Director). (1993). *The Wonderful, Horrible Life of Leni Riefenstahl.* Germany

Films:

Heck, J (Director). (2005). *The Last days of Leni Riefenstahl.* USA, New York

Riefenstahl, L (Director). (1934). *The Triumph of the Will.* Germany

Riefenstahl, L (Co-Director and writer). (1932). *The Blue Light.* Germany

Riefenstahl, L (Director). (2002) *Impressions under Water,* Germany

Riefenstahl, L (Director). *Thiefland* (1954). Germany